THE SCARIEST PLACES ON EARTH

EASTERN STATE PENITENTIARY

BY NICK GORDON

BELLWETHER MEDIA · MINNEAPOLIS, MN

Are you ready to take it to the extreme?
Torque books thrust you into the action-packed world
of sports, vehicles, mystery, and adventure. These
books may include dirt, smoke, fire, and chilling tales.
WARNING : read at your own risk.

Library of Congress Cataloging-in-Publication Data

Gordon, Nick.
Eastern State Penitentiary / by Nick Gordon.
   pages cm. -- (Torque : the scariest places on earth)
Includes bibliographical references and index.
Summary: "Engaging images accompany information about the Eastern State Penitentiary. The
combination of high-interest subject matter and light text is intended for students in grades 3 through
7"--Provided by publisher.
ISBN 978-1-60014-947-4 (hardcover : alk. paper)
1. Haunted prisons--Pennsylvania--Juvenile literature. 2. Ghosts--Pennsylvania--Juvenile literature. 3.
Eastern State Penitentiary of Pennsylvania--Miscellanea--Juvenile literature. 4. Eastern State Penitentiary
of Pennsylvania--History--Juvenile literature. I. Title.
BF1477.3.G67 2014
133.1'2974811--dc23
                                                                        2013009612

This edition first published in 2014 by Bellwether Media, Inc.

Printed in the United States of America, North Mankato, MN.

TABLE OF CONTENTS

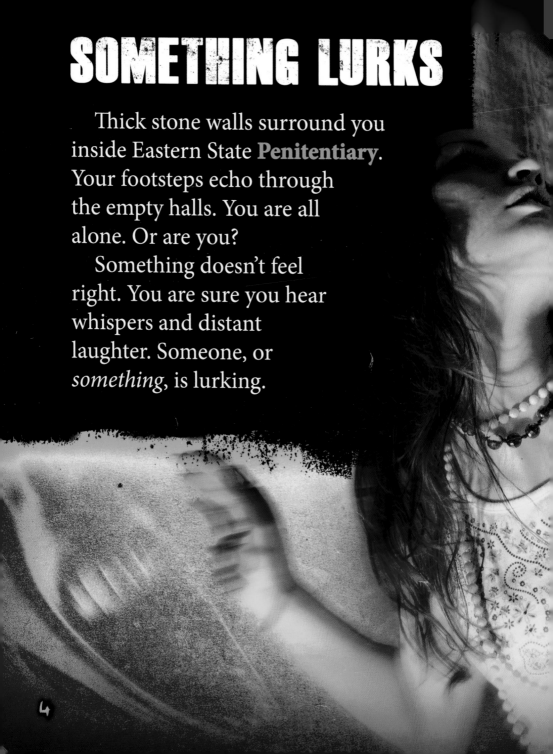

SOMETHING LURKS

Thick stone walls surround you inside Eastern State **Penitentiary**. Your footsteps echo through the empty halls. You are all alone. Or are you?

Something doesn't feel right. You are sure you hear whispers and distant laughter. Someone, or *something*, is lurking.

CHAPTER 2

A LONELY LIFE

Eastern State Penitentiary opened
in 1829 in Philadelphia, Pennsylvania.
It was built to help criminals change
their ways. **Inmates** were not allowed
to see or speak to one another. They
worked, ate, and exercised alone.
It was believed this would help them
feel **remorse** for their crimes.

THE EYE OF GOD

Each cell had a small window in the ceiling. It was called the Eye of God.

Being alone drove many inmates **insane**. In 1913, the prison began to allow shared **cells**. But prisoners faced other horrors. They were dunked in cold water and hung from a wall to freeze. Guards also strapped them to a chair for days so they couldn't move. Inmates were sometimes given just enough food to stay alive.

Many famous criminals served time at Eastern State Penitentiary. **Gangster** Al Capone spent almost a year there. Bank robber Willie Sutton was another inmate. By the 1960s, Eastern State Penitentiary was run down. Fixing it was too expensive. The prison closed in 1971.

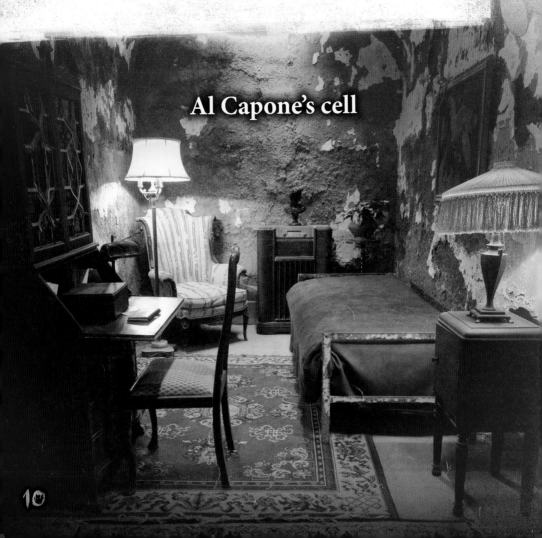

Al Capone's cell

Al Capone

Willie Sutton

TUNNELING OUT

Willie Sutton was part of a famous escape attempt. In 1945, twelve prisoners snuck out through a long tunnel they had dug. All were soon recaptured.

CHAPTER 3

HAUNTED HALLS

Guards and prisoners spoke of ghosts at Eastern before it even closed. At night, a shadowy figure has been seen at the top of a **guard tower**. It is believed to be the ghost of a guard who was murdered by an inmate. Perhaps it stands in the very spot where the guard was killed.

13

After it closed, one worker was helping to **restore** the prison. He was alone, but he felt like he was being watched. He turned. The hall was empty. He went back to work, but the feeling was still there. He turned again. A shadow leaped across the hallway.

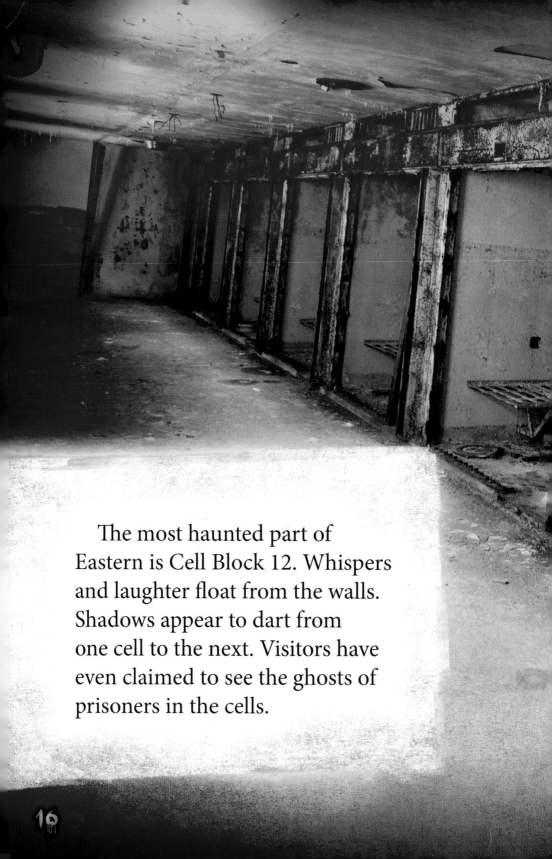

The most haunted part of Eastern is Cell Block 12. Whispers and laughter float from the walls. Shadows appear to dart from one cell to the next. Visitors have even claimed to see the ghosts of prisoners in the cells.

THE PHANTOM

One of the prison's most famous ghosts is the Phantom. Many people have seen this dark, human-like shadow. They say it gives off a feeling of anger. The figure stands in a dark corner and disappears when approached.

CHAPTER 4

RETURN FROM RUIN

Eastern remained closed for more than twenty years. Walls crumbled. Trees grew up through the floors. Then people worked to restore the prison **ruins**. The building reopened for tours in 1994. At Halloween, it turns into a giant haunted house. Brave visitors find their way through dark halls of hidden frights.

PLAYING IT SAFE

Until 2003, visitors had to wear hard hats. They wore them in case the prison walls caved in!

Ghost hunters have carefully studied Eastern State Penitentiary. They have recorded strange sights and sounds. Photos show mysterious shapes and unexplained lights. Do the ghosts of violent, insane criminals still haunt the prison today? Would you care to spend a night in the prison to find out?

GLOSSARY

cells—small rooms in which prisoners are held

gangster—a member of a gang of violent criminals

guard tower—a station set high above a prison; guards watch prison grounds from a guard tower.

inmates—people locked in a prison

insane—unable to properly understand reality

penitentiary—a prison that holds criminals found guilty of serious crimes

remorse—the feeling of being sorry for one's actions

restore—to return something to its previous condition

ruins—the remains of a human-made structure

TO LEARN MORE

AT THE LIBRARY

Chandler, Matt. *The World's Most Haunted Places*. Mankato, Minn.: Capstone Press, 2012.

Gordon, Nick. *Alcatraz*. Minneapolis, Minn.: Bellwether Media, 2014.

Hawkins, John. *Hauntings*. New York, N.Y.: PowerKids Press, 2012.

ON THE WEB

Learning more about Eastern State Penitentiary is as easy as 1, 2, 3.

1. Go to www.factsurfer.com.

2. Enter "Eastern State Penitentiary" into the search box.

3. Click the "Surf" button and you will see a list of related Web sites.

With factsurfer.com, finding more information is just a click away.

INDEX

The images in this book are reproduced through the courtesy of: Ritu Manoj Jethani, front cover (bottom), pp. 14-15; Alison Hancock, front cover (top); Croisy, front cover & p. 21 (skull); Gary Whitton, pp. 2-3 (background); Hasloo Group Production Studio, pp. 4-5 (left); Bill Dickinson/ Getty Images, pp. 4-5 (right); Associated Press, pp. 6, 11 (bottom); Asia Glab, pp. 7, 12-13, 17; Weird NJ/ Splash News/ Newscom, p. 8; Konstantins Visnevskis, p. 9; Zack Frank, pp. 10, 16; Album/ Album/ SuperStock, p. 11 (top); Dragon_fang, p. 15; Ellie Teramoto/ Alamy, p. 19; Thesab/ Creative Commons, pp. 20-21.